FINDING YOUR PURPOSE

A GUIDE TO LIVING AN AUTHENTIC LIFE

DR. JAGADEESH PILLAI

|| Dedicated to all wisdom seekers around the World ||

ॐ

Contents

Contents

Prayer

**Saraswati Namasthubhyam Varade Kamarupini
Vidyarambham Karishyami Siddhir Bavathume Sadha**

Greetings to Devi Saraswati, the benevolent granter of
blessings and fulfiller of desires. O Devi, as I embark on my
studies, I humbly ask that you grant me the wisdom to
comprehend correctly.

About The Author

Dr. Jagadeesh Pillai is a renowned Guinness World Record holder, writer, and researcher hailing from Varanasi, also known as the abode of Lord Shiva. With a Ph.D. in Vedic Science and a range of creative ideas and achievements, he is a true polymath. He is the author of more than 100 books including Research Publications. Although his roots can be traced back to Kerala, the people of Varanasi hold him in high regard and affectionately consider him one of their own.

In 1998, Dr. Pillai was offered a job at Banaras Hindu University, but he left the position after only two months to pursue greater goals in life. He believed that in order to study Indian scriptures and engage in other creative endeavours, he needed to retire from the daily grind of working solely for money at a young age.

He started an export business from scratch, using the knowledge he had gained from a previous job in the industry. His intelligence and unique approach to business led to great success in a short period of time, earning him more in just a decade and a half than he would have in a lifetime working in a government job. Upon the passing of Dr. APJ Abdul Kalam, Dr. Pillai decided to leave the business and dedicate himself to reading, studying, researching, and experimenting.

During his tenure in the export business, Dr. Pillai traveled to over 16 countries, gaining valuable insight and experiencing the world and life in detail.

Dr. Pillai has achieved four Guinness World Records in the following subjects:

"Script to Screen" - In this record, Dr. Pillai produced and directed an animation film within the shortest time possible, breaking the previous record set by Canadians. He has also received numerous national and international awards and recognitions for this achievement.

Longest Line of Postcards - For this record, Dr. Pillai created a line of 16,300 postcards on the occasion of the 163rd anniversary of Indian Postal Day. The event also included a questionnaire about the Indian flag.

Largest Poster Awareness Campaign - Dr. Pillai designed an awareness campaign on the subject of "Beti Bachao - Beti Padhao" (Save the Girl Child - Educate the Girl Child) to achieve this record.

Largest Envelope - In tribute to the Indian Prime Minister's "Make in India" initiative, Dr. Pillai created a 4000 square meter envelope using waste paper to achieve this record.

Attempted - **70000 Candles on a 210 kg Cake** - To celebrate the 70th Indian Independence Day, Dr. Pillai attempted to light 70,000 candles on a 210 kg cake, which was recorded in World Records India.

Attempted - **Documentary on Dhamek Stupa of Sarnath in 17 Languages** - Dr. Pillai attempted to create a documentary on the Dhamek Stupa of Sarnath, dubbing it in 17 different languages. The result of this attempt is currently awaiting confirmation from the Guinness World Records.

Dr. Pillai is skilled in teaching the Bhagavad Gita, a Hindu scripture, and is popular among young people. He has helped many young people improve their lives through his motivational teachings.

In addition to teaching, he has composed and sung numerous Sanskrit Bhajans and patriotic songs.

He has also written and directed several short films and documentaries for awareness campaigns, and has volunteered with the police in both UP and Kerala to spread awareness about various issues through videos and photography.

Incredibly, he has produced and directed over 100 documentaries about the city of Varanasi, all on his own.

He has also helped and guided more than 25 boys and girls to achieve world records through creative and innovative methods. He is a multifaceted person who uses his intellect and the blessings given to him by God to excel in various areas. He is both a teacher and a student, always learning and teaching, and is able to master any subject he comes across.

He is a selfless social activist and motivational speaker who has overcome struggles and failures to become a successful and enthusiastic individual with a rich life experience.

In addition to his work with the Bhagavad Gita, he is also an efficient Tarot card reader, Astro-Vastu consultant, and a talented singer and composer. He has sung the entire Ram Charita Manas and Bhagavad Gita in his own compositions, and has sung the phrase "Lokah Samastha Sukhino Bhavantu" in 50 different languages. He is currently working on a detailed and scientific study of Vedas, Upanishads, Puranas, and the Bhagavad Gita. He has also composed and sung the Hanuman Chalisa and Gayatri Mantra in 108 and 1008 different compositions, respectively.

Awards - Four Times Guinness World Records, Winner of Mahatma Gandhi Vishwa Shanti Puraskar, Mahatma Gandhi Global Peace Ambassador, Kashi Ratna Award, Dr. APJ Abdul Kalam Motivational Person of the Year 2017, Mother Teresa Award, Indira Gandhi Priyadarshini Award, Bharat Vikas Ratna Award, Udyog Ratna Award, Vigyan Prasar Award, Poorvanchal Ratn Samman.

PREFACE

Finding your purpose in life can be a challenging journey, but it is also one of the most rewarding experiences you will ever have. It is a journey of self-discovery, of learning about who you are, what you stand for, and what you want to achieve in life. It is a journey of embracing your authentic self and living a life that is true to you.

In this book, "Finding Your Purpose: A Guide to Living an Authentic Life," we will explore the various steps and techniques you can use to identify and achieve your purpose in life. We will cover topics such as understanding your values and beliefs, overcoming limiting beliefs, exploring your passions and interests, identifying your strengths and talents, clarifying your goals and dreams, developing a personal vision, and much more.

Whether you are just starting on your journey of self-discovery or have been searching for your purpose for some time, this book will provide you with the tools and guidance you need to live an authentic life filled with purpose and meaning. Our goal is to help you create a roadmap for success that is tailored specifically to your unique needs and aspirations.

So join us on this exciting journey as we explore the world of finding your purpose and living an authentic life. With determination, hard work, and the guidance in this book, you can find the purpose and meaning you have been seeking, and live the life you were meant to live.

ॐ

PREFACE

I

Introduction: Finding Your Purpose

Have you ever felt like something is missing in your life, but you can't quite put your finger on it? Do you feel like you're going through the motions each day without any real sense of direction or purpose? If so, you're not alone. Many people struggle to find their purpose in life, but the good news is that it is never too late to discover it. In this chapter, we'll delve into the concept of purpose and what it means to live an authentic life. We'll explore the different ways to uncover your purpose and the steps you can take to make it a reality.

What is Purpose?

Purpose is a sense of meaning and direction that gives your life significance. It is what drives you forward and provides a sense of fulfillment and satisfaction. Purpose is unique to each individual and can take many forms, ranging from career goals and personal ambitions to spiritual beliefs and community service. However, despite its many forms, purpose is something that all human beings share in common. It is a universal human need that provides a sense of belonging and fulfillment.

Why is Purpose Important?

Purpose is essential to living a fulfilling and satisfying life. When you have a clear sense of purpose, you are more likely to be motivated and engaged in your daily activities. This, in turn, leads to increased productivity, satisfaction, and well-being. Moreover, having a strong sense of purpose can also help you navigate life's challenges and difficulties. When you know what you stand for and what you want to achieve, you are better equipped to make decisions and overcome obstacles.

Finding Your Purpose

Finding your purpose can be a journey, but it is one that is well worth taking. The process can be different for everyone, but here are some steps that can help you on your journey:

Reflect on your values and beliefs

Start by taking some time to reflect on what is most important to you. What do you believe in? What values guide your life? When you have a clear understanding of your values and beliefs, you are better equipped to make decisions that align with your purpose.

Consider your passions and interests

What do you enjoy doing? What are you passionate about? These are often strong indicators of your purpose in life. If you're not sure what your passions and interests are, try new things and explore different areas of life. This can help you to discover what truly resonates with you.

Identify your strengths and skills

Think about what you are naturally good at and what skills you have developed over time. Your strengths and skills can be a valuable resource in helping you find your purpose. When you use your strengths and skills to make a difference in the world, you are more likely to feel fulfilled and satisfied.

Set goals

Once you have identified your values, passions, interests, and strengths, it's time to set goals. Your goals should be aligned with your purpose and should reflect what you want to achieve in your life. Write down your goals and create a plan for how you're going to achieve them.

Take action

Finally, take action towards your goals. Whether it's starting a new hobby, volunteering in your community, or pursuing a new career, taking action is the key to making your purpose a reality.

Living an Authentic Life

Once you have found your purpose, the next step is to live an authentic life. This means being true to yourself and living in a way that aligns with your values and beliefs. It means pursuing your passions and interests, and making choices that bring you happiness and fulfillment. When you live an authentic life, you are able to cultivate a deep sense of self-awareness and self-acceptance. This, in turn, leads to greater confidence, resilience, and well-being.

To live an authentic life, it's important to take care of your physical, emotional, and spiritual health. This means making time for self-care, surrounding yourself with positive and supportive people, and engaging in activities that bring you joy and peace. It also means being honest with yourself and others about your feelings, thoughts, and desires. When you are authentic, you are able to build strong and meaningful relationships with those around you.

In conclusion, finding your purpose is a journey that requires time, patience, and reflection. However, when you discover your purpose, you are able to live an authentic life filled with meaning, fulfillment, and happiness. The journey towards finding your purpose can be challenging, but the reward of living a life that is true to who you are is worth the effort. So, take the time to reflect on your values and beliefs, explore your passions and interests, set goals, and take action. And remember, your purpose is unique to you and there is no right or wrong way to find it. Embrace the journey, trust the process, and live an authentic life filled with purpose.

ಜ

"Your purpose in life is to find your purpose and give your whole heart and soul to it."

-Gautama Buddha

৪৩

II

Understanding Your Values and Beliefs

Your values and beliefs are the foundation of who you are and what you stand for. They shape your perspectives, attitudes, and behaviors, and play a critical role in determining your purpose in life. Understanding your values and beliefs is an essential step in finding your purpose and living an authentic life. In this chapter, we'll explore the concept of values and beliefs, how they shape your life, and the steps you can take to identify and understand your own values and beliefs.

What are Values and Beliefs?

Values are the things that are most important to you. They are the principles, standards, and qualities that you hold dear and that guide your actions and decisions. Examples of values include honesty, integrity, compassion, and family.

Beliefs are the convictions you hold to be true, often based on personal experiences or cultural, spiritual, or religious beliefs. They inform your attitudes, behaviors, and values and are an integral part of your identity. Examples of beliefs include a belief in God, the importance of hard work, or the value of education.

How Values and Beliefs Shape Your Life

Values and beliefs have a profound impact on your life. They shape your perspectives, attitudes, and behaviors and influence the choices you make. When your values and beliefs align with your actions, you are more likely to experience a sense of purpose, fulfillment, and well-being. On the other hand, when your values and beliefs are in conflict with your actions, you are more likely to experience feelings of frustration, dissatisfaction, and disillusionment.

Identifying Your Values and Beliefs

Identifying your values and beliefs is a critical step in finding your purpose and living an authentic life. Here are some steps you can take to identify your values and beliefs:

Reflect on your experiences and accomplishments

Think about the experiences and accomplishments that have been most meaningful to you. What values and beliefs were reflected in those experiences? Consider how those values and beliefs have shaped your life and what they mean to you.

Consider your emotions and reactions

Pay attention to your emotional reactions to different situations. What values and beliefs are being expressed in your emotions? What do those emotions tell you about what is important to you?

Explore your spirituality and/or religion

If you have a spiritual or religious background, consider how your beliefs and values are shaped by your spirituality or religion. Reflect on what you believe about the world and the purpose of life.

Ask for feedback from others

Talk to family and friends about what they see as your values and beliefs. Ask for their honest feedback and take the time to reflect on what they have to say.

Engage in self-reflection and meditation

Take time each day to reflect on your values and beliefs. Engage in self-reflection, journaling, or meditation to help you gain a deeper understanding of who you are and what you stand for.

Living Your Values and Beliefs

Once you have identified your values and beliefs, the next step is to live them. This means making choices and taking actions that align with your values and beliefs. When you live your values and beliefs, you are more likely to experience a sense of purpose and fulfillment, and less likely to feel conflicted or disillusioned.

It's important to remember that your values and beliefs may evolve over time as you gain new experiences and insights. It's okay to re-evaluate your values and beliefs and make changes as needed. The important thing is to stay true to yourself and to live in a way that is authentic and fulfilling.

In conclusion, understanding your values and beliefs is a crucial step in finding your purpose and living an authentic life. Your values and beliefs are the foundation of who you are and what you stand for, and they shape your perspectives, attitudes, and behaviors. By taking the time to identify and understand your values and beliefs, you can make choices and take actions that align with what is most important to you, resulting in greater purpose, fulfillment, and well-being. Remember, your values and beliefs may evolve over time, and it's important to stay open to change and growth. So, take the time to reflect on your values and beliefs, live them, and embrace the journey of finding your purpose.

"The only way to do great work is to love what you do."

-Steve Jobs

છ

III

Overcoming Limiting Beliefs

Limiting beliefs are negative, self-defeating thoughts that hold us back from pursuing our goals and living our best lives. They can be based on past experiences, cultural norms, or societal expectations and can limit our potential and prevent us from living an authentic life. In this chapter, we'll explore the concept of limiting beliefs, the impact they can have on our lives, and the steps we can take to overcome them.

Identifying Your Limiting Beliefs

The first step in overcoming your limiting beliefs is to identify them. This can be a difficult process, as limiting beliefs are often deeply ingrained and may be difficult to recognize. Here are some ways to identify your limiting beliefs:

Pay attention to self-talk

Pay attention to the thoughts and statements you make to yourself. Do you often say things like *"I can't do that" or "I'm not good enough"?* These types of thoughts and statements can be indicators of limiting beliefs.

Reflect on your experiences

Think about experiences in your life where you felt limited or held back. What thoughts and beliefs were present during those experiences? What impact did those beliefs have on your actions and decisions?

Consider your fears

What fears hold you back from pursuing your goals and living your best life? Fears are often rooted in limiting beliefs.

Challenging Your Limiting Beliefs

Once you have identified your limiting beliefs, the next step is to challenge them. This means taking a closer look at the beliefs and questioning their validity. Here are some steps you can take to challenge your limiting beliefs:

Ask yourself if the belief is true

Take a step back and ask yourself if the belief is actually true. Are there any facts that support the belief, or is it simply a perception or a thought?

Look for evidence that contradicts the belief

Consider any experiences or examples in your life where the belief was not true. What evidence is there to contradict the belief?

Reframe the belief

If the belief is not true, try to reframe it into a positive, empowering thought. For example, *if you believe "I can't do that", try reframing it as "I can learn and grow and be capable of doing that."*

Replacing Limiting Beliefs with Empowering Ones

Once you have challenged and reframed your limiting beliefs, the next step is to replace them with empowering beliefs. Empowering beliefs are positive, self-affirming thoughts that support your goals and aspirations. Here are some steps you can take to replace your limiting beliefs with empowering ones:

Identify your goals and aspirations

What do you want to achieve in life? What are your goals and aspirations?

Create a list of empowering beliefs

Create a list of empowering beliefs that support your goals and aspirations. For example, if your goal is to start your own business, an empowering belief might be *"I have the skills, knowledge, and creativity to succeed in starting my own business."*

Repeat your empowering beliefs daily

Repeat your empowering beliefs daily, either out loud or in your mind. The more you repeat them, the more they will become ingrained in your subconscious mind.

In conclusion, limiting beliefs can be a major obstacle in finding your purpose and living an authentic life. By identifying, challenging, and replacing your limiting beliefs with empowering ones, you can overcome these obstacles and live a life that is fulfilling and true to who you are. Remember, the process of overcoming limiting beliefs is ongoing and requires effort and determination. However, with persistence and dedication, you can develop the skills and mindset needed to live an authentic life that is true to your values and beliefs, and filled with purpose and meaning.

It's important to also be gentle and compassionate with yourself during this process. Change is not easy and it can take time, so be patient and celebrate your progress along the way. Remember, finding your purpose is a journey, not a destination, and by overcoming your limiting beliefs, you'll be taking a powerful step towards living the life you truly desire.

So, take the time to reflect on your limiting beliefs, challenge them, and replace them with empowering beliefs. With each step, you'll be closer to finding your purpose and living an authentic life that is fulfilling and meaningful.

ॐ

"The purpose of life is to live it, to taste experience to the utmost, to reach out eagerly and without fear for newer and richer experience."

-Eleanor Roosevelt

৪৩

IV

Exploring Your Passions and Interests

Discovering your passions and interests is a crucial part of finding your purpose and living an authentic life. Your passions and interests are the things that bring you joy, excitement, and fulfillment, and they are often an indicator of your purpose and what you are meant to do in life. In this chapter, we'll explore the process of discovering your passions and interests and how they can lead you towards your purpose.

Identifying Your Passions and Interests

The first step in exploring your passions and interests is to identify them. Here are some ways to do that:

Reflect on your past experiences

Think about experiences in your life where you felt particularly happy and fulfilled.

What were you doing at those times?

What were your interests and passions during those experiences?

Pay attention to your hobbies and interests

What do you enjoy doing in your free time? What hobbies and interests bring you joy and fulfillment

Consider your values and beliefs

What values and beliefs are important to you? What causes or issues do you feel passionate about?

Ask for feedback from others

Ask friends, family, and colleagues what they think your passions and interests are based on your actions, words, and behaviors.

Experiment and try new things

Don't be afraid to try new things and experiment. You never know, you may discover a new passion or interest that you never even considered before.

Pursuing Your Passions and Interests

Once you have identified your passions and interests, the next step is to pursue them. Here are some tips for pursuing your passions and interests:

Make time for them

Make time in your schedule to pursue your passions and interests, even if it's just a few hours a week. The more time you dedicate to them, the more you will be able to develop them into something more meaningful.

Find ways to incorporate your passions and interests into your daily life

Think about ways you can incorporate your passions and interests into your daily life, whether it's through your work, volunteering, or other activities.

Seek out opportunities to learn and grow

Find opportunities to learn and grow in your passions and interests, whether it's through courses, workshops, or online resources.

Surround yourself with like-minded individuals

Surround yourself with people who share your passions and interests. Joining a community or group can be a great way to connect with others who share your passions and interests.

Making Your Passions and Interests Your Purpose

Pursuing your passions and interests can lead to finding your purpose. When you're doing what you love, it can be fulfilling and meaningful, and can also provide a sense of direction and purpose in life. Here are some tips for making your passions and interests your purpose:

Reflect on your passions and interests

Reflect on your passions and interests and think about how you can turn them into a career or a larger purpose.

Research opportunities

Research opportunities in your passions and interests, whether it's through careers, volunteer work, or entrepreneurial ventures.

Take action

Take action towards your passions and interests. Start small and build up gradually. Don't be afraid to take risks and make changes in your life to pursue your passions and interests.

In conclusion, exploring your passions and interests is a critical part of finding your purpose and living an authentic life. By taking the time to identify, pursue, and make your passions and interests your purpose, you'll be taking a significant step towards living a life filled with joy, fulfillment, and meaning. Don't be afraid to experiment and try new things, and always be open to new opportunities that align with your passions and interests.

Remember, finding your purpose is a journey, not a destination, and it's never too late to start exploring your passions and interests. Take the time to reflect on what brings you joy, and don't be afraid to make changes in your life to pursue them. By doing so, you'll be living an authentic life that is true to who you are and what you value.

In summary, exploring your passions and interests is a key aspect of finding your purpose and living an authentic life. By taking the time to identify, pursue, and make your passions and interests your purpose, you'll be on your way to a life filled with meaning, joy, and fulfillment.

"The meaning of life is to find your gift. The purpose of life is to give it away."

-Pablo Picasso

೮౩

V

Identifying Your Strengths and Talents

Identifying your strengths and talents is another important step in the journey of finding your purpose and living an authentic life. When you understand what you're naturally good at and what you enjoy doing, you can begin to use those strengths and talents in service of a larger purpose. This can bring a sense of fulfillment and satisfaction that comes from using your unique skills and abilities to make a positive impact in the world.

There are many ways to identify your strengths and talents. One popular method is to take a strengths assessment test, which can help you understand your natural tendencies and tendencies. You can also reflect on times in your life when you felt a strong sense of satisfaction and fulfillment, and try to identify the skills and activities that were involved. Pay attention to what comes naturally to you, and what you enjoy doing without much effort.

Another way to identify your strengths and talents is to think about the feedback you've received from others throughout your life. What have people complimented you on or thanked you for? What have they said you're really good at? This feedback can give you important insights into your strengths and talents.

It's important to remember that your strengths and talents are not set in stone, and that you can continue to develop and expand them over time. Take the time to reflect on your strengths and talents, and identify areas where you'd like to grow and improve. Consider taking courses, workshops, or finding a mentor to help you develop your skills further.

Once you've identified your strengths and talents, it's important to put them to use in a way that aligns with your values, passions, and interests. When you're using your strengths and talents in service of something you care deeply about, you'll be able to tap into a deeper sense of purpose and fulfillment.

In conclusion, identifying your strengths and talents is a crucial step in the journey of finding your purpose and living an authentic life. When you understand what you're naturally good at and what you enjoy doing, you can use those strengths and talents to make a positive impact in the world and live a life filled with meaning and fulfillment.

"The only way to discover the limits of the possible is to go beyond them into the impossible."

-Arthur C. Clarke

ॐ

VI

Clarifying Your Goals and Dreams

Clarifying your goals and dreams is a vital part of the journey to finding your purpose and living an authentic life. Having a clear understanding of what you want to achieve, both in the short-term and the long-term, can give you direction and focus as you navigate the ups and downs of life. It can also help you prioritize your time and resources so that you can make the most of your journey.

The first step in clarifying your goals and dreams is to set aside time for reflection and introspection. Take a moment to think about what you truly want in life, both in the near future and in the long term. Consider your values, passions, interests, and strengths, and think about how they can be integrated into your goals and dreams.

Next, try to be specific about your goals and dreams. For example, instead of simply saying "I want to be happy," try to think about what specific actions or experiences will bring you happiness. Similarly, instead of saying "I want to be successful," try to think about what success means to you, and what specific steps you need to take to achieve it.

It's also important to make your goals and dreams achievable and realistic. While it's important to aim high and challenge yourself, setting goals that are too far out of reach can lead to disappointment and frustration. Consider breaking down large goals into smaller, more manageable steps, and take the time to celebrate each accomplishment along the way.

Finally, it's important to make your goals and dreams visible. Write them down, or create a vision board, to help keep them front and center in your mind. This can also help to hold yourself accountable, and keep you motivated and inspired as you work towards your goals.

In conclusion, clarifying your goals and dreams is a critical part of the journey to finding your purpose and living an authentic life. By taking the time to reflect on what you truly want, and making your goals and dreams achievable and visible, you'll be able to stay focused, motivated, and inspired as you navigate the ups and downs of life.

"The purpose of life is not to be happy. It is to be useful, to be honorable, to be compassionate, to have it make some difference that you have lived and lived well."

-Ralph Waldo Emerson

෮

VII

Developing a
Personal Vision

Developing a personal vision is an important step in finding your purpose and living an authentic life. A personal vision is a clear and compelling picture of the future you want to create for yourself. It encapsulates your values, passions, interests, strengths, and goals, and provides a roadmap for your journey towards a fulfilling life.

The first step in developing your personal vision is to clarify your values, passions, interests, and strengths. As you reflect on these elements, try to envision a future in which they are all fully integrated into your life. What does your life look like when you are living in alignment with your values and passions? What kind of work do you do, and what kind of relationships do you have?

Next, consider your long-term goals and dreams. What do you want to achieve in your career, your relationships, and your personal life? How do these goals fit into the overall picture of your life, and what kind of impact do you want to have on the world?

Once you have a clear sense of your values, passions, interests, strengths, goals, and dreams, it's time to start piecing together your personal vision. Try to articulate this vision in a way that is meaningful and inspiring to you. Consider using visual aids, such as a vision board or a collage, to help you bring your vision to life.

It's important to note that your personal vision will evolve over time. As you grow and change, your vision will change with you. This is why it's important to revisit your vision regularly, and make updates as needed.

In conclusion, developing a personal vision is a critical step in finding your purpose and living an authentic life. By taking the time to clarify your values, passions, interests, strengths, and goals, and by envisioning a future in which they are all integrated into your life, you'll have a roadmap to guide you as you navigate the ups and downs of life. So take the time to develop your personal vision, and start living the life you truly want to live.

"The purpose of life is to contribute in some way to making things better." a

-Robert F. Kennedy

ೞ

VIII

Establishing a Meaningful Career

Establishing a meaningful career is a key aspect of living an authentic life. When you're doing work that aligns with your values, passions, interests, and strengths, you're more likely to feel fulfilled and satisfied. However, finding a career that is truly meaningful can be a challenge, especially in today's fast-paced and competitive world.

The first step in establishing a meaningful career is to get clear on your values, passions, interests, and strengths. As you reflect on these elements, try to envision a career in which they are all fully integrated. What kind of work do you find most fulfilling, and why? What are you naturally drawn to, and what makes you feel most alive?

Next, consider your long-term goals and aspirations. What kind of impact do you want to have on the world, and how can your career help you achieve this impact? What kind of lifestyle do you want to have, and how can your career support this lifestyle?

Once you have a clear sense of your values, passions, interests, strengths, goals, and aspirations, it's time to start exploring career options. This might involve conducting informational interviews, networking with people in your desired field, taking on internships or volunteer work, or even enrolling in classes or workshops to develop new skills. It's also a good idea to gather information about the job market and industry trends, so that you can make informed decisions about your career path.

It's important to note that establishing a meaningful career is not a one-time event, but rather a ongoing process. As you grow and change, your career will change with you. This is why it's important to revisit your career goals regularly, and make adjustments as needed.

In conclusion, establishing a meaningful career is a critical aspect of living an authentic life. By getting clear on your values, passions, interests, and strengths, and by exploring career options that align with these elements, you can find work that is truly fulfilling and satisfying. So take the time to establish a meaningful career, and start living the life you truly want to live.

"The purpose of life is to live it with courage, grace, and authenticity."

-Oprah Winfrey

രു

IX

Creating a Positive Mindset

Creating a positive mindset is a key aspect of living an authentic life. When you have a positive outlook on life, you're more likely to be resilient, optimistic, and confident, which can help you overcome challenges and achieve your goals. Unfortunately, many people struggle with maintaining a positive mindset, especially when faced with obstacles or setbacks.

The first step in creating a positive mindset is to cultivate awareness of your thoughts and emotions. Take time each day to reflect on what you're thinking and feeling, and notice how these thoughts and emotions impact your overall well-being. When you become aware of negative thoughts or emotions, make a conscious effort to shift your perspective to a more positive one.

Next, practice gratitude on a daily basis. Focus on what

you have, rather than what you lack, and take time to acknowledge and appreciate the good things in your life. Whether it's a simple act of kindness from a stranger, or a beautiful sunset, make a conscious effort to savor the positive experiences in your life.

Another effective way to create a positive mindset is to engage in physical exercise and self-care. When you take care of your body, you feel better both physically and mentally. Regular exercise can boost your energy levels, reduce stress, and improve your overall mood. In addition, engaging in self-care activities, such as meditation, yoga, or taking a relaxing bath, can help you unwind, de-stress, and cultivate a sense of inner peace.

It's also important to surround yourself with positive, supportive people. Seek out relationships with individuals who bring out the best in you, and who are genuinely interested in your well-being. Avoid toxic people and relationships that drain your energy, and instead focus on building healthy, meaningful relationships with those who inspire and uplift you.

Finally, focus on personal growth and self-improvement. Engage in activities and experiences that challenge you, and push you to grow and evolve as a person. This might involve learning a new skill, traveling to a new place, or tackling a difficult project. The key is to keep pushing yourself, and to stay open to new experiences and opportunities.

In conclusion, creating a positive mindset is a critical aspect of living an authentic life. By becoming aware of your thoughts and emotions, practicing gratitude, engaging in physical exercise and self-care, surrounding yourself with positive people, and focusing on personal growth and self-improvement, you can cultivate a positive outlook on life and achieve greater happiness and well-being.

"The purpose of life is to live it with intention. To love deeply and laugh wildly."

-Mandy Hale

ଃ

X

Crafting an Authentic Personal Brand

Crafting an authentic personal brand is an essential step in finding your purpose and living an authentic life. A personal brand is not just a visual representation of who you are, but also a reflection of your values, beliefs, and goals. By creating a personal brand, you are able to communicate your unique value proposition to the world and attract opportunities that align with your purpose.

The first step in crafting your personal brand is to get clear on who you are and what you stand for. Take time to reflect on your values, beliefs, strengths, and passions, and determine what sets you apart from others. Consider what message you want to convey about yourself, and what sets you apart from others in your field.

Next, think about your target audience and what they are looking for. What are their needs, values, and pain points? How can you address these needs and provide value to your target audience? By understanding your target audience, you can tailor your personal brand to meet their needs and build a strong, meaningful connection with them.

Once you have a clear understanding of who you are and what your target audience needs, you can start to develop your personal brand. This involves creating a visual representation of your brand, such as a logo or tagline, as well as developing a consistent message and tone across all of your communications and interactions.

Your personal brand should also be reflected in your online presence. Consider how you present yourself on social media, your personal website, and other online platforms. Ensure that your messaging is consistent and that you are presenting yourself in a professional, authentic manner.

In addition to your online presence, it's important to actively promote your personal brand in person as well. Attend networking events, speak at conferences, and engage in other activities that allow you to build relationships and share your brand with others.

Finally, it's important to continuously refine and evolve your personal brand as you grow and change over time. Regularly reflect on your values, beliefs, and goals, and make adjustments to your personal brand as needed to ensure that it remains aligned with who you are and what you stand for.

In conclusion, crafting an authentic personal brand is a critical component of finding your purpose and living an authentic life. By getting clear on who you are, understanding your target audience, creating a visual representation of your brand, promoting your brand online and in-person, and continuously refining and evolving your brand over time, you can effectively communicate your unique value proposition to the world and attract opportunities that align with your purpose.

"The purpose of life is to live it with passion and purpose."

-Tony Robbins

છ

XI

Cultivating Self-Leadership

Cultivating self-leadership is a crucial step in finding your purpose and living an authentic life. Self-leadership involves taking charge of your own thoughts, emotions, and behaviors, and using them to achieve your goals and aspirations. It is about being accountable for your own life and taking responsibility for your own success.

The first step in developing self-leadership is to become aware of your thoughts and emotions. This means paying attention to the self-talk that goes on in your mind and recognizing when negative or self-defeating thoughts arise. Once you become aware of these thoughts, you can challenge and reframe them in a more positive and empowering way.

Next, focus on developing a growth mindset. This means embracing challenges as opportunities for growth, and viewing setbacks and failures as opportunities to learn and improve. By adopting a growth mindset, you will be able to bounce back from challenges more quickly and overcome obstacles that may have previously held you back.

In addition to developing a growth mindset, it's important to establish clear, achievable goals. This involves setting specific, measurable, time-bound goals that align with your purpose, and creating a plan to achieve them. By having clear goals, you will be able to focus your energy and effort in the right direction and make steady progress towards your aspirations.

Self-leadership also requires developing strong personal habits that support your goals and aspirations. This may involve establishing a consistent exercise routine, practicing mindfulness and meditation, and developing healthy eating habits. By taking care of your physical and mental well-being, you will be better equipped to handle the challenges that come with pursuing your purpose.

Finally, cultivate self-awareness by regularly reflecting on your thoughts, emotions, and behaviors. Ask yourself questions such as: "What am I doing well?" "What do I need to improve?" "What do I need to do differently?" By regularly reflecting on your self-leadership skills, you will be able to identify areas for improvement and make changes as needed.

In conclusion, cultivating self-leadership is essential to finding your purpose and living an authentic life. By becoming aware of your thoughts and emotions, adopting a growth mindset, setting clear goals, developing strong personal habits, and regularly reflecting on your self-leadership skills, you will be able to take charge of your life and achieve your aspirations. Self-leadership is not a one-time event, but rather a continuous journey of growth and development. By embracing this journey, you will be well on your way to finding your purpose and living an authentic life.

"The purpose of life is to live it with courage, to embrace the adventure, and to never stop growing."

-John C. Maxwell

ॐ

XII

Building Healthy Relationships

Building healthy relationships is an important aspect of finding your purpose and living an authentic life. Relationships with family, friends, and romantic partners provide a supportive network that can help you achieve your goals and aspirations. At the same time, relationships can also be sources of stress and conflict that can hinder your progress.

One key to building healthy relationships is to practice effective communication. This means listening actively to others, expressing your thoughts and feelings in a clear and non-judgmental manner, and resolving conflicts in a respectful and cooperative way. Good communication skills can help build trust and mutual understanding in your relationships, and can prevent misunderstandings and conflicts from escalating.

It's also important to establish clear boundaries in your relationships. This means setting limits on what you are willing to tolerate from others, and being assertive in communicating your needs and expectations. By having clear boundaries, you will be able to maintain your sense of self in your relationships and avoid feeling overwhelmed or taken advantage of.

Another aspect of building healthy relationships is to engage in activities that bring you joy and bring you closer to the people you care about. This could be anything from taking a walk in the park to cooking dinner together to traveling to a new place. By sharing experiences with others, you will be able to deepen your connections and create memories that will last a lifetime.

It's also important to cultivate empathy and compassion in your relationships. This means putting yourself in others' shoes, understanding their perspectives, and treating them with kindness and respect. By showing empathy and compassion, you will be able to build strong, supportive relationships that are based on mutual understanding and respect.

Finally, it's important to seek out and surround yourself with positive, supportive people who share your values and aspirations. This may involve seeking out new friends or joining groups and organizations that align with your interests. By surrounding yourself with supportive people, you will be able to find encouragement, inspiration, and a sense of community as you pursue your purpose.

In conclusion, building healthy relationships is a crucial

aspect of finding your purpose and living an authentic life. By practicing effective communication, establishing clear boundaries, engaging in activities that bring you joy, cultivating empathy and compassion, and surrounding yourself with positive, supportive people, you will be able to build a supportive network that will help you achieve your goals and aspirations. Remember, relationships are a two-way street, and the effort you put into building healthy relationships will be reflected in the quality of the relationships you have in your life.

"The purpose of life is to live it with joy and purpose, to make a difference in the world, and to leave a legacy."

-Les Brown

ॐ

XIII

Developing a Growth Mindset

One of the keys to finding and living your purpose is having a growth mindset. A growth mindset is the belief that your abilities, intelligence, and talents can be developed and improved through effort and learning. It is the opposite of a fixed mindset, where you believe your abilities are set and cannot be changed.

A growth mindset can help you overcome challenges, pursue your passions and interests, and continuously grow and evolve as a person. Here are a few ways to develop and maintain a growth mindset:

Embrace challenges: When faced with challenges, view them as opportunities to learn and grow. Don't be afraid to fail and make mistakes, as they are opportunities for growth and improvement.

Focus on the process, not just the outcome: Instead of solely focusing on the end goal, focus on the journey and the steps you take to get there. Celebrate small wins and progress along the way.

Seek feedback and criticism: Ask for feedback and criticism from trusted sources, and use it to grow and improve. Don't be defensive or take it personally, instead, see it as a tool for growth.

Be open to learning: Always be open to learning and trying new things. Read books, attend workshops, and seek out new experiences. This will help you continue to grow and evolve.

Practice gratitude: Cultivate a habit of gratitude and focus on the positive. Appreciate your growth and progress, no matter how small it may be.

Having a growth mindset is a crucial aspect of finding your purpose and living an authentic life. By embracing challenges, focusing on the process, seeking feedback, being open to learning, and practicing gratitude, you can develop a growth mindset and continuously grow and evolve.

Remember, the journey of finding your purpose is ongoing and always evolving. Embrace the journey and be open to new experiences and growth opportunities. With a growth mindset, you will be able to live an authentic life and achieve your goals and dreams.

"The purpose of life is to live it with courage to take risks, to be creative, and to never give up.

-Oprah Winfrey

ॐ

XIV

Embracing Life's Challenges

One of the key aspects of living an authentic life is embracing life's challenges. Life is full of obstacles, but it is how we respond to them that determines our growth and success. Challenges can help us build resilience, deepen our character, and develop a sense of purpose. In this chapter, we will explore why embracing challenges is essential for living an authentic life, and provide practical strategies for doing so.

Why Embracing Challenges is Important

Challenges are an inevitable part of life, and it is how we approach them that can make all the difference. When we embrace challenges, we become more resilient and better equipped to handle the ups and downs of life. Challenges can also help us grow and develop new skills, build self-esteem, and deepen our character.

Furthermore, embracing challenges can help us clarify our values, beliefs, and purpose. When we face challenges, we are forced to think deeply about what is most important to us, and what we stand for. This can lead to a greater sense of self-awareness and a clearer understanding of our personal values and beliefs.

Strategies for Embracing Challenges

Reframe your mindset: When faced with a challenge, it can be easy to feel overwhelmed and defeated. However, reframing your mindset can make a big difference. Instead of viewing challenges as insurmountable obstacles, try to see them as opportunities for growth and personal development.

Embrace failure: Failure is a natural part of the growth process, and it is essential to embrace it. When we embrace failure, we are better able to learn from our mistakes, and avoid making the same mistakes in the future.

Seek support: Embracing challenges can be difficult, and it can be helpful to seek support from friends, family, or a support group. Having someone to talk to about your experiences can provide a sense of comfort and validation, and can help you stay motivated.

Stay positive: It can be easy to get discouraged when facing challenges, but it is important to maintain a positive outlook. Surrounding yourself with positive people and activities can help you stay motivated, and can provide a sense of hope and inspiration.

Celebrate your successes: When you overcome a challenge, it is important to celebrate your successes. This can help you build self-esteem, and can provide a sense of accomplishment and satisfaction.

Embracing life's challenges is an essential part of living an authentic life. When we face challenges with resilience, determination, and a positive mindset, we can grow and develop in meaningful ways. By reframing our mindset, embracing failure, seeking support, staying positive, and celebrating our successes, we can navigate life's obstacles with grace and confidence. With time and practice, you will be better equipped to handle life's challenges, and to live an authentic and fulfilling life.

The purpose of life is to live it with passion, to make a positive impact, and to never stop learning.

-Ralph Waldo Emerson

৪৩

XV

Living with Intention and Purpose

Living with intention and purpose is about aligning your actions and decisions with your core values, beliefs, passions, interests, and goals. It means being present and mindful in the moment, and taking deliberate steps towards creating a life that brings you fulfillment and satisfaction. When you live with intention and purpose, you become the master of your life, rather than simply reacting to external circumstances.

To live with intention and purpose, you must first be clear on what you want to achieve and why. Ask yourself questions like: What are my goals and aspirations? What brings me joy and fulfillment? What kind of impact do I want to make in the world? Having a clear understanding of what you want will help you focus your efforts and make informed decisions that support your overall vision.

Next, you must cultivate a growth mindset and be open to change. Embracing life's challenges is an important part of personal growth, and can help you gain a deeper understanding of yourself and your purpose. Whether it's a small setback or a major obstacle, viewing challenges as opportunities for growth will help you stay focused and motivated.

In addition to a growth mindset, it's also important to develop strong self-leadership skills. This means being accountable for your thoughts, feelings, and actions, and taking responsibility for your life. When you lead yourself, you have the power to create the life you want, and you're able to navigate the ups and downs of life with grace and resilience.

Building healthy relationships is also critical to living with intention and purpose. Surrounding yourself with supportive and encouraging individuals will help you stay motivated and on track towards your goals. At the same time, it's important to be mindful of the relationships that may be holding you back, and to make changes where necessary.

Finally, living with intention and purpose requires a positive mindset and a commitment to self-improvement. This means actively seeking out opportunities for growth, learning, and development, and investing in yourself on a regular basis. When you make a commitment to personal growth, you open yourself up to new possibilities and experiences, and you become better equipped to pursue your goals and live a fulfilling life.

In conclusion, living with intention and purpose is about creating a life that aligns with your core values, beliefs, passions, interests, and goals. It requires a clear understanding of what you want, a growth mindset, strong self-leadership skills, healthy relationships, and a commitment to personal growth. When you live with intention and purpose, you become the master of your life, and you experience a sense of fulfillment and satisfaction that comes from living authentically.

The purpose of life is to live it with love, to be kind to others, and to always strive for excellence.

-Mother Teresa

ଚଠ

OTHER BOOKS OF THE AUTHOR

൭

Contact

DR. JAGADEESH PILLAI

MBA & PhD in Vedic Science

Four Times Guinness World Record Holder

Winner of Mahatma Gandhi Vishwa Shanti Puraskar and Global Peace Ambassador

Gemology, Astro & Vastu Consultant - Spiritual Counselor

Consultant for designing World Record Ideas

Efficient Tarot Card Reader

9839093003

myrichindia@gmail.com

drjagadeeshpillai@facebook

drjagadeeshpillai@instagram

jagadeeshpillai@youtube

www. JAGADEESHPILLAI.com

ൖ

|| LOKAHA SAMASTHAHA SUKHINO BHAVANTU ||

ಶ್ರೀ

CPSIA information can be obtained
at www.ICGtesting.com
Printed in the USA
BVHW041415040623
665300BV00001B/49

9 798889 751724